KAZ COOKE

Warning:
contains
Big, Fat
Lies.

PENGUIN BOOKS

Penguin Books

Published by the Penguin Group
Penguin Books Australia Ltd
250 Camberwell Road, Camberwell, Victoria 3124, Australia
Penguin Books Ltd
80 Strand, London WC2R 0RL, England
Penguin Putnam Inc.
375 Hudson Street, New York, New York 10014, USA
Penguin Books, a division of Pearson Canada
10 Alcorn Avenue, Toronto, Ontario, Canada M4V 3B2
Penguin Books (NZ) Ltd
Cnr Rosedale and Airborne Roads, Albany, Auckland, New Zealand
Penguin Books (South Africa) (Pty) Ltd
24 Sturdee Avenue, Rosebank, Johannesburg 2196, South Africa
Penguin Books India (P) Ltd
11, Community Centre, Panchsheel Park, New Delhi 110 017, India

First published by Penguin Books Australia Ltd 2003

10 9 8 7 6 5 4 3 2 1

Text and illustrations copyright © Kaz Cooke 2003

The moral right of the author has been asserted

Designed by Nikki Townsend, Penguin Design Studio
Typeset in Officina Sans Book by Nikki Townsend, Penguin Design Studio and Post Pre-press, Brisbane
Printed and bound in Australia by McPherson's Printing Group, Maryborough, Victoria

National Library of Australia
Cataloguing-in-Publication data:

Cooke, Kaz, 1962– .
The little book of excuses.

ISBN 0 14 300167 1.

1. Excuses – Humor. I. Title.

A828.302

www.penguin.com.au

Yes, I know I said I'd never write
another Little Book, but . . .

The wombat ate my homework.

The photocopier was on the blink.*

*Possibly because my bottom was on it.

My car wouldn't stop.

My goldfish is psychotic.

I thought you were dead.

The instruction manual is in Urdu.

I had an unusual flu that temporarily stripped me of the competent control of my bodily functions.

My pants were unusually tight.*

*Originally used by a misfielding baseballer,

but potentially of much wider use.

I must have blacked out.
Either that or my skivvy was
stuck on my head.

Ohmigod . . . I . . . I can't
remember who I am!

The devil made me do it. He wore
red pantihose, and everything.

I don't know what came over me.*

*Although stupidity is a possibility.

I was abducted by aliens.
They probed my mind, hid the
car keys and waxed my legs.

It may seem like I was selfish,
but actually everything I do,
I do it for you-ooo-ooo.

I care more about the money
than our friendship.

I've always wanted to wear
a spangled stripper's outfit.

My mother wouldn't let me.
She's been dead for 17 years, but
I'm sure she wouldn't let me.

I lost my leg in a threshing
incident.*

*For best results use only on the phone.

I had temporary Tourette
syndrome and couldn't stop
shouting 'Slut puppy!'
for no reason.

My ferret is missing.

My dog has laryngitis.

I was attacked by a giant
preposition just outside my gate.

I ate my alarm clock.

I have a flat tyre, and I lent my
spare tyre to a friend who was
making a swing.

I was too shickered to breathe.

I've just been diagnosed with
terminal concupiscence.*

*This actually means wanting
something badly.

But didn't you *ask* me last
Thursday to smash that vase
and be enormously rude to
all the clients?

My car wouldn't start. I think it has something to do with the fact that I don't have a car.

I had to wait until my
nail polish dried.

All my underpants were
in Botswana because of a
service-wash mix-up.

I think I'm dead, but I'll call
you tomorrow and let you
know when I'm sure.

I'm deadlocked inside the house
and my wife has gone away
for three days.

I can't leave the house
because there is a vicious magpie
dive-bombing every passer-by
and I don't have an ice-cream
container with eyes drawn
on the back of it.

I am with the Army Reserve
and this afternoon we are
invading Corsica.

My budgie has lice.

I'm in Las Vegas and I'm pretty
sure I just married this
cocktail waitress.
What's your name, honey?

I have Women's Trouble.
When that's over I fully expect
to have a bout of Person Trouble.

I have massive diarrhoea. It's just pouring out of me and it's kinda green and has this chunky . . . (continue until other person begs you to stop).

I thought it was daylight saving.

I thought it was the end of
daylight saving.

What's daylight saving?

I was having sex with a fireman.
Okay, I was *dreaming* about
having sex with a fireman.

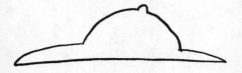

I'd love to sleep with you, but
your wife would kill me.

If I didn't have bacterial scurvy
I'd be there in a flash.

I just saw on a documentary that Curvaceous Lemurs are the most dangerous animal in the world, and I'm pretty sure there's one on my verandah.

I'm waiting for the test results,
but they're pretty sure I've got
non-specific morbid dread.

It's nothing personal.
It's just that I'm only really
sexually interested in people
wearing gigantic furry
animal suits.

This morning there was a huge electrical storm and I was struck by a coincidence.

I was so drunk I threw up in my
handbag and my underpants are
on somebody's windscreen.

I'm suffering third degree burns
from my Brazilian bikini wax.

I was captured by the Borg
and was reliably informed that
resistance was futile.

My axolotl died.
Of course I'm sure. I shot it.

There is a boiled egg
stuck in my ear.

I have to wait for the
incoming tide.

Normally I'm very calm, but
I had just had some red cordial
and a Polly Waffle.

I'd love to, but I have to
shampoo my toenails.

I think about you constantly.
It's just that I'm not good
with names.

There's a huge wad of
lime-green bubblegum stuck
in my pubic hair.

I would love to help with the
housework but you're so good
at it, it's like watching the
creation of art. Another beer
would be good.

I would, but I'm a Pisces.

My brother was using the pencil.

Of course I'm straight.
I'm simply going to a Streisand
film marathon on Saturday.

I can't leave the house because
I had cosmetic surgery on
the weekend and now I look
like Melanie Griffith.

At the time, I was captain of the
Australian cricket team and
I just couldn't get away.

I'm an Olympic shooter and
I can't have sex the night before
I shoot those little clay thingies,
for my country.

I'm allergic to exercise.

I would go for a run, but I don't
want to frighten my lungs.

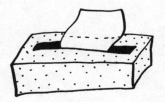

It may seem like I was speeding,
but there was a rent in the
space-time continuum.

I was at the meeting.
It's just that I thought it
was in Istanbul.

Of course I am not drunk.
You cannot get drunk on
crème de menthe frappés.

Well, obviously, if you're going to have 'red' lights that particularly repellent shade of cerise you can't expect people to take them seriously.

How dare you question
my morals? They are extremely
expensive.

My girlfriend sent me out saying
not to come home without
some Malibu, but I thought
she said caribou, and now
I'm in Alaska.

I had to wax the catboat.

I was giving birth to twins.

I am in a film with
Robert Downey Jr.

It was a performance art piece:
I was getting a rash from
the leotard.

:shrug: :shrug:

Psychologically, it's important
for me to be late so that you
feel more strongly about
wanting me to arrive.

The reason my toddler is
spooning food into your briefcase
is that we're trying self-regulation.
It certainly seems to work in the
nuclear industry.

It's just so complicated to keep
track of where my sperm goes.

I didn't. I wouldn't. It was HER.

I might've

I was going to turn up to the church but there was a really good repeat on of *Antiques Roadshow* in Latvian.

I am currently the object of
a large land, air and
sea search.

I can't come because I forgot
I was going on a pub crawl
with a bloke called Barry.

All the lonely Tim Tams in the packet were missing their friends in my tummy.

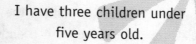

I have three children under
five years old.

My guinea pig stole my glasses
and now I'm legally blind.

er

I didn't come home in April
because I had some overtime.

I hit every red light on the way
here (and now the car is
covered in dents).

oops

I believe myself to be
a small amphibian.

I fell over in the shower
and a lemon went up my bottom.

I am being guided by the spirit
voices of my dead relatives
channelled by that smarmy TV
guy. And they say, don't go to
work today, and eat a two-kilo
tub of ice-cream.
What's that dead relatives?
And watch videos all day?
Well, okay, if you insist.

I haven't got a thing to wear.
Except this baby doll dress
with a spangly G-string
and platform thongs, with
a rubber bathing cap.

My temperature is 58 degrees.

I got a truly disastrous perm
and can't leave the house
for two months.

My sideburns caught fire.

I couldn't get out of the house
because of the bad feng shui.

I had a guacamole fight and some got up my nose, so I'm waiting in Casualty.

There is a bandicoot in my carburettor and, as they are endangered, I have to wait for it to come out.

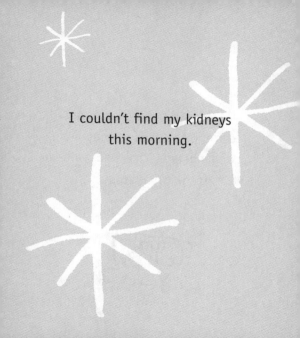

I couldn't find my kidneys
this morning.

The batteries in my magic wand
wore out.

There was a water shortage,
so I bathed in martinis.

It is a Total Fire Ban today and
my car runs on wood.

I can't just have one drink.
I have a medical condition that
means I have to have
36 drinks.

I thought you really wanted to
know whether your arse
looked fat in that.

My bosoms have a mind of
their own.

I've got worker's block.

I thought it was an RDO:
Ridiculous Day Off.

Of course I can keep a secret.
It's just more fun to give
them away.

..... secrets

I have sesquipedalism.*

*A tendency to use long words.

I shouldn't have started
screaming, but I've never seen
one as small as that.

How was I to know the lift would stop if I smashed the control panel with a house brick?

I can't possibly have made these purchases. I don't like clothes, music or food.

I have mange.

My credit card has a mind
of its own.

flap flap

VISA
4503 723211

It may have seemed to you that
I was dancing licentiously, but I
merely had an itchy foot.

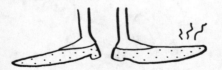

I don't know why you won't believe me. I've worked for days on that excuse.

If I didn't hit you with a cudgel,
I was going to stab you with
a butter knife.

I'd love to help you, but I'm actually quite spectacularly self-centred.

I needed the drugs more than you
needed your CD collection.

It wasn't plagiarism, it was postmodern free-form research methods.

Do I know you?
(Always a good one with
close relatives.)

I fell off my platform shoes.

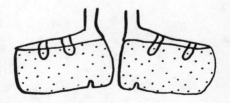

I'm just not myself.
(Possibly I'm Zsa Zsa Gabor.)

I got a lot of calls after I put my husband on eBay.

I was at my Caribbean steel drum
band and sinuous pogo lesson.

It's not that I don't find you
enchanting, it's just that
you remind me of
Ernest Borgnine.

We had musical differences.
I wanted to go in a more mature
direction, and they are big fat
stinky pooheads.

Things seemed to be escalating, so I thought it would be more reassuring if I shouted 'Run! For the love of GOD, RUN FOR YOUR LIVES!'

It's not a sinister moustache, it is
a smear of squid ink I received
during a hand-to-hand fight
with a bosun.

That didn't happen.
And if it did happen, I'm amazed
and appalled that you could be
so base as to bring it up.

It's not like we're having
a relationship. We just go out
together, share meals
and have sex.

Guilt is not a useful emotion.
It's far more positive to do what
you want and feel like you've
got off scot-free.

I was auditioning for a
Village People tribute band
under strong lights and the
construction hat got fused to
my head with burning feathers.

I toppled over into a flaming pit
of writhing serpents without
my mobile phone.

My wallet is going hungry and
I left my baby on the train.*

*Used by a guy asking for $35 in the street.

There was a bottle of VB in the pram.

I can't eat wheat, eggs, meat, fish, dairy, commercially produced vegetables, non-organic fruit, cultivated nuts, or grains from the earth. So just a sliver of steamed polystyrene for me, thanks.

I already ate – it was
something last April.

I want to spend more time with my wife and children, just as soon as I can remember their address.

But you see, where I come from
'Shut your face you skanky troll'
is a compliment of the
highest order.

If only I could get my wallet out
of my pocket – but my arm has
developed an asingular
ulnar formation.*

*That's a normal forearm bone.

Damn. I must have left my wallet
in my other life.

Nobody could be more surprised than me, but apparently I am sort of Elvish Queen and impervious to earthly criticism.

Well if you don't want people
washing their hair with it, you
shouldn't leave birthday present
French champagne wrapped up in
the fridge in the first place.

I thought you liked
rubber spiders.

I have a tendency to isochronal bipedal vectitation.*

ooh

*Walking using both feet.

I get confused when you can't
even make up your mind.
I mean, do you want to know
where I was, or do you want
to know if I slept with
someone else?

Eddie McGuire is blocking my driveway and I can't get out.

I thought it was faux baby seal.

It isn't you. It's me. Or maybe
that guy over there.
For all I know the president
of Uzbekistan probably has
something to do with it.

Think of it this way: if you love
something, set it free.
Then, if it comes back to you,
you can slap it and throw its
clothes into the street.

I'm sorry I'm late, but I was involved in an unscheduled counter-terrorist insurgency near the cosmetics counter.
Either that or it was a lipstick demonstration.

Is that the time?

But when you said you wanted
a classy string quartet, I thought
you wanted me to book Mental As
Anything singing *Smoke on the
Water* in cockney accents.

My pants, as it happens,
are on fire.

Kaz Cooke is the author of many best-selling books including **The Little Book of Stress**, **The Little Book of Crap** (with Simon Weaselpantz), **The Little Book of Dumb Feng Shui**, **The Little Book of Beauty**, **The Little Book of Household Madness** and **The Little Book of Diet and Exercise**. Large books include **Up the Duff** (about pregnancy) and **Kidwrangling: Caring for Babies, Toddlers and Preschoolers**. She was going to write another book this week but her brother borrowed the pencil.

www.kazcooke.com